Some time ago, a well-known national publication announced a search for innovative solutions to three global problems (including global health problems). The application said **"Tell us about the problem you are inspired to solve."** Here's what I said:

Children with mental illness symptoms need practice using new, mature problem-solving strategies and tactics. Seeing a counselor once or twice a week in their office will never be enough practice for the vast majority of children! Parents and teachers don't have the skill, patience, time or ability to deliver all of the practice opportunities that children with disabilities (Autism, ADHD) require to learn new skills successfully. Professionals who are trained and supervised can do this.

Then, they said **"Provide a clear sense of how your idea will solve the problem identified."**
Here's what I said:

I0418845

A single licensed mental health professional can train and closely supervise 10 or more Masters-level mental health professionals who in turn each train and supervise 9 or more Bachelors-level professionals who deliver behavioral support and therapeutic guidance (opportunities to practice new skills) in the child's own home, school and community. No trips to an office, ever. The services are entirely "evidence based" treatment procedures with decades of success behind them. And they're free.

Finally, they said **"Share what inspired you to create your idea."** Here's what I said:
I'm a licensed psychologist and a certified school psychologist in Pennsylvania with 40 years of experience. My staff and I have been delivering treatment to children using the model I created and described above, with funding for 20, 30 or more hours of intensive, individualized treatment weekly per child. We've treated hundreds and hundreds of children successfully with this model.

Over the past 35 years, the staff of the Institute for Behavior Change and I have been perfecting the treatment model I created when I was a newly licensed psychologist in 1981. That treatment model, which I call *Effective Treatment in a Wraparound Cup*® has been examined by independent researchers from four different educational institutions since 2007. They all agree that the results are remarkable and worthy of publication. With well over 1,000 treatment plans studied, they reported that the probability that the positive changes they found in the lives of the children we treated had occurred due to *chance* was less than **one in ten thousand**. That's called a powerful and "statistically significant" finding in the professional literature, but not everybody respects findings like that, so I continue to call attention to the good work we're doing to the best of my ability.

This book contains the results of some recent treatment outcome research and showcases the treatment outcome measurement system that I developed over the past 20 years that has been so successful in helping to obtain and retain behavioral treatment funding for children via the EPSDT mandate of the Medicaid Act. I call it The Kossor Scale. It has uses far beyond mental health treatment, for sure.

Thanks to my family and to all of the wonderful children, parents and staff I've met over the years. Best wishes always for future success and happiness, with hope and courage abounding*!*

Steve

The Kossor Scale for Treatment Outcome Measurement

Published by Night Stage Productions, Inc.

www.NightStageProductions.com

NIGHT STAGE PRODUCTIONS

The Kossor Scale for treatment outcome measurement

The measurement of treatment outcome is crucial to the development and implementation of a treatment program in any discipline. Unless treatment delivery personnel know where they're hoping to go, they can't evaluate the course of treatment and can stray from the path that they intended to take. Some mental health treatment delivery personnel manage this challenge by not describing their intended destination explicitly. By giving only vague statements about "creating outcomes of social significance," they give themselves as much freedom to claim success as possible, no matter what happens to the child being treated. Obviously, it is important for professional treatment providers to know their client's pre-treatment experiential milieu before they start implementing any treatment program; this is called "baseline" recording. Once a baseline has been recorded, a professional mental health treatment provider can design a treatment plan that makes sense on paper and can be described to the people who will fund it, and can be implemented with high fidelity by the people who will deliver it. Without a written treatment plan, treatment delivery personnel are simply taking advantage of "regression toward the mean" (things will get better over time if they're pretty awful now) or other functions that have nothing to do with the treatment plan or how well it was delivered.

The treatment plan has to be developmental. It's not appropriate to start with "D" then go to "F" and then to "B" in an alphabetic continuum of options. The progression of treatment has to make sense given the developmental characteristics of the child who is receiving treatment. Children are different, but not so much so that just one (1) and only one (1) treatment plan alone will be helpful to them. As Harry Stack Sullivan said in 1947 *"We are all simply more human than otherwise"* so a few basic components are essential, no matter who is being treated or whatever the condition that is being addressed.

1. The treatment plan has to be written down so that it can be implemented *with fidelity.*

2. Treatment providers have to be trained so they can implement the plan *with fidelity*.

3. Treatment outcome must be measured *throughout* the treatment delivery because

4. Clients will respond to the treatment, positively or negatively, on an ongoing basis, so

5. The treatment plan has to be amended when it starts to derail (which is inevitable).

6. The recipient of treatment has to be involved in the outcome measurement, because *only they* can determine the quality of life that the treatment plan has created.

7. The providers of treatment should also be measuring treatment outcome on an ongoing basis so that *both* treatment provider and recipient agree on the outcome being created.

The Kossor Scale for Treatment Outcome Measurement was developed between 1996 and 2019 to achieve these seven objectives. By incorporating the input of both treatment providers and treatment recipients (or their parents if the recipients are young children), standardized measures of both the *frequency* and the *severity* of identified target behavior were created. Aberrant "target behavior" was operationally defined in *binary* terms (so that it could be rated as present or absent), which translated directly into a comprehensible treatment plan.

Properly trained professionals who were closely supervised by other adequately trained, resourceful professionals implemented the plan with fidelity. This allowed the treatment providers and the parents of the treatment recipients to record whether a "target behavior" occurred with nearly 100% accuracy.

Replacement (good) behavior emerged with increasing frequency and intensity as the aberrant behavior diminished, and was measured by other scales (including norm-referenced measures) in conjunction with the Kossor Scale, which is a criterion-referenced measure. Such measures are commonly used in school classrooms to measure student progress in learning a curriculum that is defined by an individual teacher for his/her current students.

The Kossor Scale has been described as "an annotated Likert *(LIK-ert)* scale," but this is inaccurate because a Likert scale uses a continuum that is *generically* defined, usually having five points, and where the characteristics of one point are only *generally* related to those of adjacent points.

For example, an opinion poll is often designed as a Likert scale:

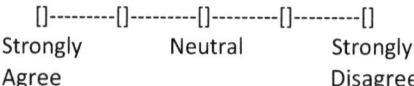

| []---------[]---------[]---------[]---------[] |
| Strongly   Neutral   Strongly |
| Agree   Disagree |

In comparison, the Kossor Scale has the following characteristics:

- 10 points define the continua for each of *two* companion scales, scored simultaneously:
    - frequency
    - severity
- Each point is explicitly defined and is explicitly related to the adjacent points
- Each of the points describes a set of conditions unique to that point on the continua
- Aberrant "target behavior" is operationally defined in objective, *binary* terms, either:
    - The aberrant behavior did occur
    - The aberrant behavior did not occur

By following these principles, recording errors are minimized and the treatment plan itself can be written in language that directs treatment providers to respond to particular events in particular ways. As the results of their interventions are recorded, the trajectory of the treatment program is defined. Necessary adjustments can promptly be made to correct the trajectory so that aberrant behavior reduces while adaptive "replacement behavior" increases.

Like all Criterion Referenced measures, the Kossor Scale measures the life experience of a particular individual whose behavior is being monitored within the context of a particular experiential milieu. Norm Referenced measures compare the performance of the monitored person with the performance of other "similarly situated" persons from a "normative group" – none of whom is experiencing the same particular experiential milieu.

Norm-referenced measures have enjoyed wide recognition within the behavioral literature, but criterion-referenced measures provide a perspective that norm-referenced measures simply cannot.

It is helpful to have both Norm Referenced measures (CARS-2, BASC-3, Vineland-3, CANS, ADOS, ATEC, etc.) in addition to at least one Criterion Referenced measure in the evaluation of a child's treatment program if the aim is to evaluate the *quality of life* that the treatment produces. It is clear that norm-referenced measures are not sensitive to relatively small changes over relatively short periods of time.

However, criterion-referenced measures can be exquisitely sensitive to such changes if the target behavior is defined in sufficiently objective (i.e., binary) terms. The Kossor Scale for treatment outcome measurement can be applied with ease to treatment of <u>any</u> sort (podiatry, for example) where a measure of quality-of-life is sought. It excels as a parental assessment of progress for a child's behavioral treatment program.

The treatment provider has to construct a treatment plan with statements operationally defining aberrant target behavior in binary terms ("kicking others" for example). The supervisor of the treatment program has to interview the treatment recipient (or their parent if they are very young) once weekly as to their impression of the frequency and severity of the operationally defined target behavior. By recording the ratings of the treatment *recipient* (or their single designated representative) on a set schedule, a Single Subject with Repeated Measures experimental design is implemented.

When the supervisor of the treatment program *interacts* with the rating provider during the data collection process (comparing previous ratings with current ratings), both the reliability and the validity of the Kossor Scale can approach 100%. Moreover, in the course of implementing treatment outcome measurement with the Kossor Scale, the perspectives of the treatment recipient and the treatment provider necessarily move closer together and result in a more consistent and satisfactory treatment delivery process. Here is an example of the Kossor Scale used to evaluate the treatment outcome of a behavioral treatment plan for a child:

The Kossor Scale for treatment outcome measurement – child behavior Frequency rating

Frequency Ratings: **IN THE PAST WEEK** the target aberrant behavior occurred …

0-1 **Nonexistent (0)** or **virtually nonexistent - less than once in a month and not worrisome (1)**

 2 Upper limit of normal (tolerable) for a child of the same approximate age

3-4 A <u>few</u> times in the past week, *almost* **every week in the past month (3)** to *every* **single week (4)**

5-6 <u>Many</u> times in the past week, *almost* **every week in the past month (5)** to *every* **single week (6)**

7-8 Several times daily (breaks in-between incidents), *almost* **every day (7)** to *every* **single day (8)**

9-10 Constantly (stops only briefly before restarting), *almost* **every day (9)** to *every* **single day (10)**

The preceding scale can be adapted to address the behavior of an adult. It can also be adapted to measure the display of any aberrant behavior or symptom presentation whatsoever. The treatment provider simply needs to construct a continuum of frequencies between "nonexistent" and "constantly" and use clearly demarcated time frames for each of the points in-between.

A score of 0 or 1 defines the frequency of a functionally absent component. It is either not happening at all (0), or is so rare (1) that it is functionally absent from the life experience of the person whose treatment outcome is being measured. Likewise, in the Severity scale to be described shortly, a score of 0 or 1 defines a severity that has either no effect whatsoever (0), or has an effect so minimal that it is functionally ineffectual (1) in the life experience of the person whose treatment outcome is being measured. Each score on the 1-10 continuum of the Kossor Scale has a corresponding description that allows the rater to identify that score, to the exclusion of all others, as the single best score to match their perception of the frequency and severity of the behavior being assessed.

The Kossor Scale for treatment outcome measurement – child behavior Severity rating

Severity Ratings: **IN THE PAST WEEK** the target aberrant behavior was ......

0-1 The behavior is not worrisome. There are *no* **(0)** or *almost* **no (1)** negative consequences imaginable.

2 Upper limit of normal (tolerable) for a child of the same approximate age. Typically developing children of the same approximate age who you know are displaying behavior at this level and it doesn't warrant professional attention. It is manageable, but may be very frustrating at times.

3-4 The child's behavior is severe enough to worry you, *almost* **every time** (3) to *every* **single time** (4). Behavior isn't responding to the "usual" interventions that work with typically developing children of the same approximate age who you know. Behavior requires outside help to manage or change. It is **not obviously** *hurting* the child or others, but if it *persists*, it will **probably** result in someone getting hurt, or the child is failing to be successful in meeting life's challenges.

5-6 You characterize the child's behavior as very serious, *almost* **every time** (5) to *every* **single time** (6). Outside help has been involved in the past and hasn't helped, or isn't consistently helping now, but there are more "good days" than "bad days" overall. Behavior *is* **hurting** the child or others when it happens, but it requires no more than "first aid" and no professional medical attention. If it *persists* or gets worse, it will **certainly** result in a need for professional medical attention.

7-8 You characterize the child's behavior as alarmingly serious, *almost* **every time** (7) to *every* **single time** (8). There are relatively more "bad days" than "good days" overall. Behavior results in a need for professional medical attention above the level of "first aid" (including an Emergency Room visit to treat a relatively minor injury without hospital admission), **no suicidal or homicidal intent is apparent** and **the child was never missing from an assigned area.**

9-10 You characterize the child's behavior as catastrophic because it was, or is potentially, life-threatening. A rating of 9 would mean that nobody died and the child's behavior did not *appear* to be intended as a suicidal or homicidal act, or that an Emergency Room visit was necessary to treat a serious injury but **did** *not* **result in a hospital admission** (of the child or anyone else), or that **the child was missing** from an assigned area **for** *up to* **15 minutes.** Special Incident Report required. MMCO notification may be necessary.

A rating of 10 would mean that a successful or thwarted suicidal or homicidal act has occurred, or that an Emergency Room consultation resulted in a **hospital admission** (of the child or anyone else), or that the child was in some other **life-threatening situation**, that the **child was missing** from an assigned area for *more than* 15 minutes (over 4 hours requires MMCO notification). Special Incident Report required.

It is not possible for a score on the Kossor Scale to be assigned to more than one instance of a given behavior. This is true because the treatment outcome "target behavior" is defined in binary terms and neither they, nor the rating scales used to measure them overlap; they are all *mutually exclusive*.

A score of 2 in this example is defined as "the upper limit of normal (tolerable) for a child of the same age." Thus, *biting objects* might be rated "2" for a one-year old child who is teething, whereas a "3" or higher would be appropriate for a five year-old who is doing the exact, same thing. The severity ratings are divided into 10 discrete intervals *that do not overlap*. The Kossor Scale uses a Behavior Record Form to collect these data so that they can be viewed easily and recorded efficiently, rather like a section of "movie film" recording a series of images.

Behavior Record Form

Child's Name: *LN*, *FN*   MAID #: *MAID*

Target #1: *Target1 operational*
Target #2: *Target2 operational*
Target #3: *Target3 operational*

Frequency Ratings: 0-1 nonexistent 2 Upper limit of normal for age 3-4 several times/wk 5-6 many times/wk 7-8 several times/day 9-10 constantly
Severity Ratings: 0-1 utterly benign 2 Upper limit of normal for age 3-4 enough to worry you 5-6 very serious 7-8 alarmingly serious 9-10 catastrophic

Once each week record the *rater*'s ratings about frequency and severity of the target behavior below.

Date (mm/dd/yyyy)	Target #1			Target #2			Target #3		
	Frequency	Severity	Average	Frequency	Severity	Average	Frequency	Severity	Average

BSC Collecting Data: *BSC*   Person Supplying Information:

Each week, the frequency and severity ratings are recorded on the Form and an average is computed for each target behavior domain. Target behavior is operationally defined at the top of the form so that the rater and the treatment provider are both *exactly* aware of the behavior that is being measured (not just the domain within which the target behavior exists).

The treatment provider describes the target behavior explicitly in a binary fashion in the Operational Definition. Physical aggression might be operationally defined as "hitting, kicking and spitting" and these would be understood to refer to acts directed against a person (not an object). Spitting on the floor would not constitute "physical aggression" but spitting on (or at) a *person* would.

Defining target behavior in this explicit way makes it possible for treatment providers to focus conscientiously on improving treatment *delivery* and to apply *treatment outcome measurements* consistently. These are two essential components of Applied Behavior Analysis (ABA).

Applied Behavior Analysis in action – *Effective Treatment in a Wraparound Cup*®

The staff I supervise at The Institute for Behavior Change have been delivering Behavioral Health Rehabilitation Services (BHRS, still mistakenly called "wraparound services" in Pennsylvania) to children under the age of 21 who are disabled and enrolled in Medicaid since 1997.

The BHRS model I developed infuses "Full Fidelity Wraparound" methodology with Applied Behavior Analysis (ABA) procedures to deliver *Effective Treatment in a Wraparound Cup*® in homes, schools and other community settings under the scope of practice of licensed professional psychologists. At least one parent (or guardian) must be *actively* involved in the planning and delivery of our BHRS program.

The staff take outcome data *every week* from parents and use those data to improve the quality of the treatment process on an ongoing basis, in accordance with the evidence-based standards of ABA and Wraparound practice. A written Treatment Plan that describes and controls the child's treatment program is always developed with input from the child, parent(s), teacher(s) and other adults who have roles in the child's life. The child's strengths, weaknesses, and treatment needs are reviewed on an ongoing basis by a Masters-level Behavior Specialist who consults with parents (and others, if necessary) at least once weekly to record data about the child's progress.

A Bachelors level Therapeutic Staff Support (TSS) provider is usually assigned to work directly with the child to implement the child's treatment plan on an intensive, one-to-one basis for several hours each week.

A Mobile Therapist may meet with the child at home, in school, or elsewhere in the community to provide psychological counseling on one or more occasions each week. The Mobile Therapist and Behavior Specialist may also meet with the child's teachers, extended family members, or other adults who interact with the child, so that all adults in the child's life can work collaboratively toward the attainment of the treatment plan's goals. A licensed psychologist assumes full and complete professional responsibility for all services provided.

The Questionnaire shown below was developed to facilitate the reliable collection of data. If the person receiving treatment is a child, the parent should be interviewed. Although a teacher or other caretaker can certainly supply these data, it is strategically preferable to obtain outcome data **from the parent** because an insurance company functionary is much less likely to publicly malign the intentions (or capacity) of a parent as a supplier of reliable or valid information about the child's condition.

Kossor Scale Weekly Questionnaire

Client Name: _____   DOB: _____

Date: _____

Person providing response: Parent   Other caretaker (specify): _____

Has the child's insurance changed?   No   Yes*

If you circle yes, please take a picture of the new insurance card and submit to administration as soon as possible. If the insurance has changed and client has an ASD diagnosis, a new Act 62 questionnaire is also needed.

Assessor: I will now ask questions about [behavior]. Remember, examples of [behavior] include: [examples]. Take a moment to think about just last week, and specifically about how often behavior associated with [behavior] occurred *in the last week*.

Which best describes [behavior]?

		Frequency Ranking:		Score
1		Does not occur		0
2		Has not occurred in the last month		1
3		Has occurred only a few times in the last month		2
4		Has occurred *some* (under half) of the weeks in the month		
	4a	During the weeks [behavior] has occurred, did it happen *on more than half of the days* during that week.	No	3
			Yes	5
5		Has occurred *most* (over half) of *weeks* in the month		
	5a	During the weeks [behavior] has occurred, did it happen *on more than half of the days* during that week.	No	4
			Yes	6
6		Has occurred *most* (over half) of the *days* in the month		7
7		Has occurred *every single day* in the last month		
	7a	Which best describes the behavior:	Not Constantly	8
			Constantly, with short pauses	9
			Constantly	10

8

The second half of the Kossor Scale addresses the severity of the child's behavior, and the following Questionnaire was developed to facilitate the reliable collection of data in that domain. Again, the parent should be the respondent, rather than a service provider or other caretaker, as a strategy, to minimize the probability of data dismissal.

Kossor Scale Weekly Questionnaire

Take a moment to think about the last week, and specifically about how worrisome the behavior associated with [behavior] was *only in the last week.*

Which best describes [behavior]?

		Severity Ranking:		Score
1		I can manage the behavior without professional help.		
	1a	Does the behavior cause:	No worries at all	0
			Almost no worries at all	1
			Some worries, but nothing that needs professional attention.	2
2		Enough to worry me and I need some professional help, but not pretty serious		
	2a	The behavior causes me to have this level of worry…	Sometimes and other times it isn't as bad.	3
			Every time it occurs	4
3		Pretty Serious		
	3a	The behavior is serious and causes me to worry more than a little about it…	Sometimes and other times it isn't as bad.	5
			Every time it occurs	6
4		So serious that the behavior results in injuries that require medical attention		
	4a	The behavior results in injuries…	Only sometimes	7
			Every time it happens	8
5		Catastrophic and life-threatening		
	5a	Which best describes the behavior?	The behavior has put my child's or another person's life in jeopardy	9
			The behavior has injured my child or someone else's to the point of hospitalization or incarceration.	10

Duration Ranking:

How long was the longest episode of [behavior] in the last week?

Score Sheet

	Frequency	Severity	Max Duration
Behavior 1			
Behavior 2			
Behavior 3			

It is important to understand what the term "Applied Behavior Analysis" (ABA) means. In the field of mental health treatment, unfortunately, for every expert, there seems to be "an equal and opposite expert." As a result, the definitions of "ABA" are varied and sometimes contradictory, and can be misapplied to self-serving purposes.

What is Applied Behavior Analysis (ABA)?

Applied Behavior Analysis (ABA) is the science of controlling and predicting human behavior. Behavior analysts reject the use of hypothetical constructs and focus on the observable relationship of behavior to the environment. By functionally assessing the relationship between a targeted behavior and the environment, the methods of ABA can be used to change that behavior. Research in applied behavior analysis ranges from behavioral intervention to basic research that investigates the rules by which humans adapt and maintain behavior.

Areas of Application

ABA-based interventions are best known for treating people with developmental disabilities, most notably autism spectrum disorders. However, applied behavior analysis contributes to a full range of areas including: AIDS prevention, conservation of natural resources, education, gerontology, health and exercise, industrial safety, language acquisition, littering, medical procedures, parenting, seatbelt use, severe mental disorders, sports, and zoo management and the care of animals.

Definition of ABA

ABA is defined as the science in which the principles of the analysis of behavior are applied systematically to improve socially significant behavior, and in which experimentation is used to identify the variables responsible for change in behavior. It is one of the three fields of behavior analysis. The other two are behaviorism, or the philosophy of the science; and experimental analysis of behavior, or basic experimental research.

Other definitions of ABA exist, for example:
http://encyclopedia.thefreedictionary.com/applied+behavior+analysis
but Baer, Wolf, and Risley's 1968 article is still used as the standard description of ABA. It describes the seven dimensions of ABA: application; a focus on behavior; the use of analysis; its technological, conceptually systematic, effective, and general approach.

Characteristics of ABA

Baer, Wolf, and Risley's seven dimensions are:

- **Applied**: ABA focuses on areas that are of social significance. In doing this, behavioral scientists must take into consideration more than just short-term behavior change, but also look at how behavior changes can affect the person being treated (client), those who are close to the client, and how any change will affect the interactions between the two.

- **Behavioral**: ABA must be behavioral, i.e.: behavior itself must change, not just, what the consumer *says* about the behavior. It is not the goal of the behavior scientists to get their consumers to stop complaining about behavior problems, but rather to change the problem behavior itself. In addition, behavior must be objectively measured. A behavior scientist cannot resort to the measurement of non-behavioral substitutes.

- **Analytic**: The behavior scientist can demonstrate believable control over the behavior that is being changed. In the lab, this has been easy as the researcher can start and stop the behavior at will. However, in the applied situation, this is not always easy or ethical. Two experimental designs are particularly useful in applied settings: *reversal* and *multiple baseline* designs. The reversal design is one in which the behavior of choice is measured prior to any intervention. Once the pattern appears stable, an intervention is introduced, and behavior is measured.

  If there is a change in behavior, measurement continues until the new pattern of behavior appears stable. Then, the intervention is removed or reduced, and the behavior is measured to see if it changes again. If the behavioral scientist truly has demonstrated control of the behavior with the intervention, the behavior of interest should change as the intervention changes.

- **Technological**: This means that if any other researcher were to read a description of the study, that researcher would be able to "replicate the application with the same results." This means that the description must be very detailed and clear. Ambiguous descriptions do not qualify.

  A good check for the technological characteristic is to have a person trained in applied behavior analysis carefully read the description and then act out the procedure in detail. If the person makes any mistakes, adds any operations, omits any steps, or has to ask any questions to clarify the written description then the description is not technological and requires improvement.

- **Conceptually Systematic**: A defining characteristic is that research must be conceptually systematic by only utilizing procedures and interpreting results of these procedures in terms of the principles from which they were derived. Invocation of unobservable mediating conditions is eschewed as unnecessary in the language of behavior analysis.

- **Effective**: An application of these techniques improves behavior under investigation. Specifically, it is not the theoretical importance of the variable, but rather the practical importance (social importance) that is essential. Interventions produce *outcomes of social significance*, not just changes in behavior.

- **Generality**: The new behavior should last over time, in different environments, and spread to other behaviors not directly treated by the intervention. In addition, continued change in specified behavior after intervention for that behavior has been withdrawn is also an example of generality.

In 2005, Heward, et al., added their belief that the following five characteristics should be added:

- **Accountable**: Direct and frequent measurement enables analysts to detect their success and failures to make changes in an effort to increase successes while decreasing failures. ABA is a scientific approach in which analysts may guess but then critically test ideas, rather than "guess and guess again." This constant revision of techniques, commitment to effectiveness and analysis of results leads to an accountable science.

- **Public**: Applied behavior analysis is completely visible and public. This means that there are no mystical, metaphysical or magical claims underlying the causes of behavior. Thus, ABA produces results whose explanations are available to all of the public.

- **Doable**: ABA has a pragmatic element in that implementers of interventions can consist of a variety of individuals, from teachers to the participants themselves. This does not mean that ABA requires one simply to learn a few procedures, but with the proper planning, it can effectively be implemented by most everyone willing to invest the effort.

- **Empowering**: ABA provides tools to practitioners that allow them to change behavior effectively. By constantly providing visual feedback to the practitioner on the results of the intervention, this feature of ABA allows clinicians to assess their skill level and builds confidence in their technology.

- **Optimistic**: According to several leading authors, practitioners skilled in behavior analysis have genuine cause to be optimistic for the following reasons:

  - The environmental view is essentially optimistic as it suggests that all individuals possess roughly equal potential.

  - Direct and continuous measurements enable practitioners to detect small improvements in performance that might have otherwise been missed

  - As a practitioner uses behavioral techniques with positive outcomes, the more they will become optimistic about future success prospects.

  - The literature provides many examples of success teaching individuals considered previously "unteachable."

Because the *Effective Treatment in a Wraparound Cup*® model of BHRS I developed combines Full Fidelity Wraparound methodology with ABA principles and practices, it creates the most effective mental health treatment delivery modality possible for children in their homes, schools and communities. Independent researchers at UNC - Chapel Hill (2007) and Thomas Jefferson University (2010) found statistically significant associations between the delivery of BHRS by our staff and reductions in physical aggression, lack of environmental safety, noncompliance with adult prompts, communication deficits and socialization deficits in more than 1,000 treatment plans for children between 2 and 19 years of age.

Effective Treatment
... in a wraparound cup®

University of North Carolina at Chapel Hill   July 2007

PROMISING TREATMENT FOUND FOR CHILDREN

WITH INAPPROPRIATE BEHAVIOR

Researchers Natasha K. Bowen, Ph.D. and Erica Richman, MA at the University of North Carolina at Chapel Hill studied 301 treatment records of children age 3 to 17 between 2002 and 2007. They found that Behavioral Health Rehabilitation Services (BHRS) implemented by the staff of the Institute for Behavior Change had a statistically significant association with reductions in physical aggression, socialization deficits, noncompliance with adult prompts and communication deficits.   An association was also found with improvements in environmental safety. These results were obtained after just four months of treatment in children who had not received prior mental health treatment. Because there was no comparison group, no claims of causality can be made, but consistent findings of association between interventions and outcomes is promising.

Thomas Jefferson University, Philadelphia   July 2010

PROMISING TREATMENT CONFIRMED

FOR CHILDREN WITH INAPPROPRIATE BEHAVIOR

Researcher Staci Perlman, Ph.D. of Thomas Jefferson University in Philadelphia studied 887 treatment records of children age 3 to 19 between 2002 and 2010 and discovered that Behavioral Health Rehabilitation Services (BHRS) delivered by the staff of the Institute for Behavior Change were associated with highly significant reductions in the display of physical aggression, noncompliance with adult prompts, socialization deficits, communication deficits & lack of safety awareness. Because there was no comparison group, no claims of causality can be made, but the large number of cases studied and findings consistent with those of previous research shows that the BHRS model created by licensed psychologist Steven Kossor has remarkable promise for treating children with Autism, ADHD & other serious behavioral challenges. The probability that these results are due to chance is less than 3 in 1,000 for all five of the behavioral domains analyzed.

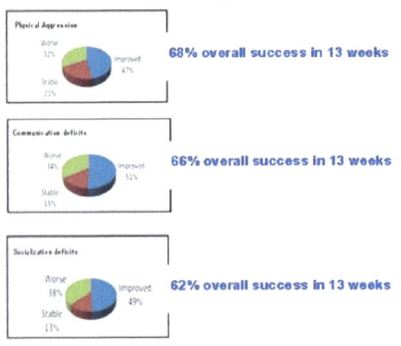

68% overall success in 13 weeks

66% overall success in 13 weeks

62% overall success in 13 weeks

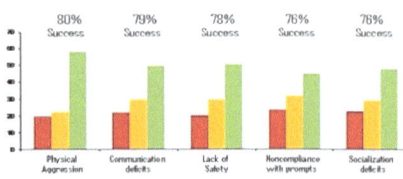

887 treatment programs

over 75% significantly improved or stabilized

in one year or less

Other researchers from Villanova University (2012) and Immaculata University (2013) found comparable evidence, summarized by the truism **"You can't drive a tack with a toothpick."**

- ## Overall improvement in all categories p<.0001
- Race, gender, family income – **all made no difference**
- Children with Autism, ADHD and Impulse Control Disorders had the greatest improvements
- BHRS was not helpful if very low levels were delivered

You can't drive a tack with a toothpick.

- Children responded **individually** to *individualized* treatment
- Higher BHRS hours (over 15 hrs/week) resulted in greater improvements in communication skills for ASD children.
- Longer BHRS terms resulted in greater improvements in physical aggression.

The data from the Behavior Record Form is projected onto the Behavior Record Graph shown below. When these data are plotted correctly, and annotated by the treatment provider, a clear understanding of the interaction between the child and the treatment program emerges. An example of a completed Behavior Record Graph is shown on the cover of this little book and in a much more readable format on the next page.

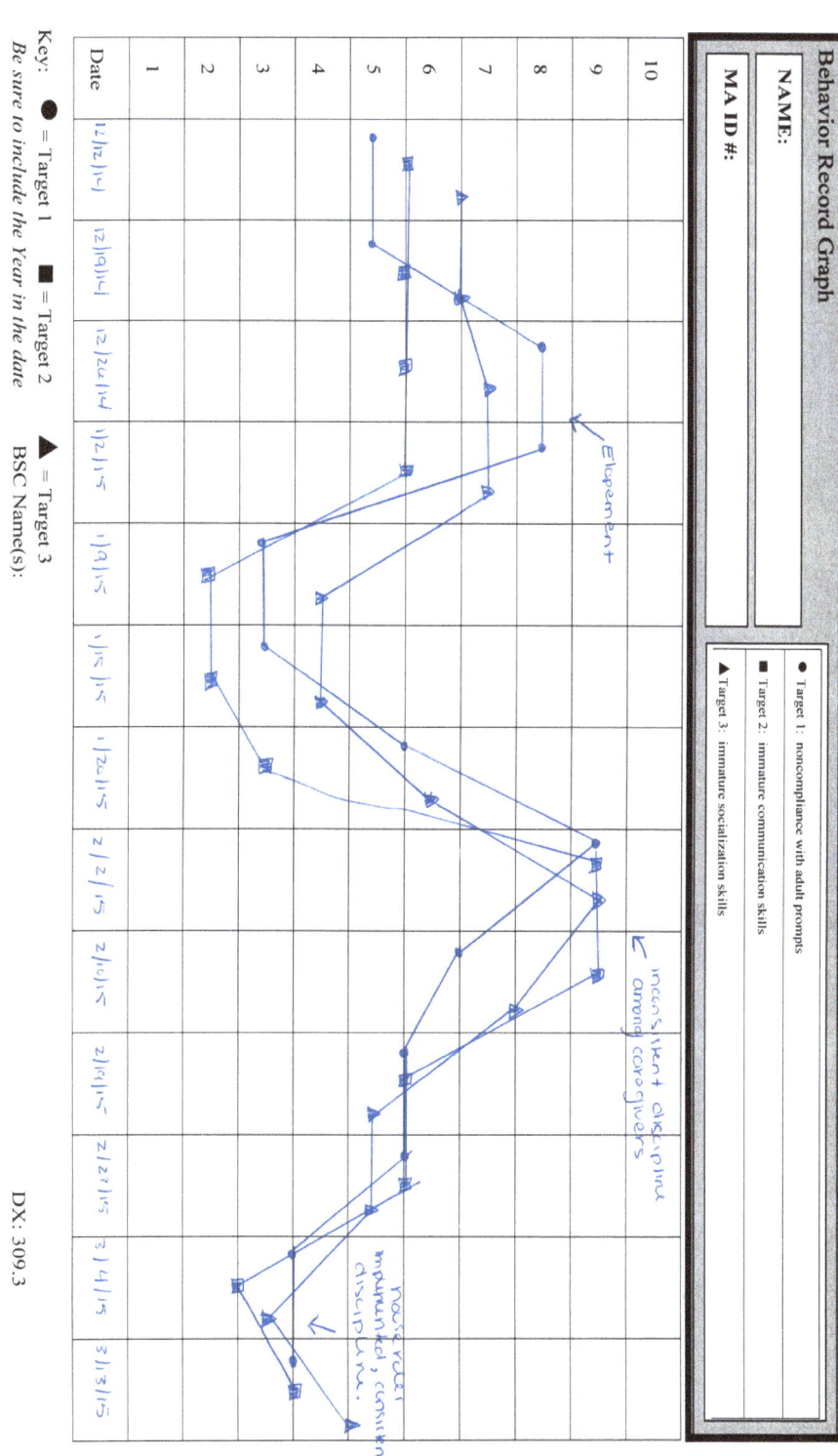

Discharge Planning

It is widely understood among ethical treatment professionals that discharge planning has to begin as part of the process of admitting someone into a treatment program. They understand that the discharge plan has to be a *written* statement that establishes the criteria for discharge from treatment. They understand that when those criteria are met, treatment should be concluded because it has achieved the goals for which it was implemented. The discharge plan used by the staff of the Institute for Behavior Change incorporates the Kossor Scale and provides a very clear understanding that, in the treatment of children, **the parent's report of progress** is the foundation upon which discharge planning is conducted. If the parent believes that their child has met the criteria for discharge from treatment, future funding for that treatment program will almost certainly become unavailable, as it should. By the same token, if the parent's report of progress shows that the child continues to display aberrant behavior in excess of the level displayed by typically developing children of the same approximate ate, it is *almost impossible* for a funding agency to reduce or eliminate Early and Periodic Screening, Diagnosis and Treatment (EPSDT) funding. The reader is referred to The Issachar Project (Kossor, 2016) for a thorough review of EPSDT funding.

Transition Planning

A clever way that funding agencies use to reduce or eliminate necessary treatment is to claim that "naturally occurring resources" can and should take-over the responsibility for **teaching** new skills to the child, not just help the child practice those skills. The argument goes that these "naturally occurring resources" must be involved treatment delivery so that the skills of the treatment professional can "transfer" to these "naturally occurring resources" who will then take-over the responsibility for teaching the child, as if that is just the most "natural" thing in the world to do. There is nothing "natural" about providing expert mental health treatment to a child with a disability. It is difficult, demanding and exacting *work*. It can be emotionally rewarding if it's done conscientiously and with proper support from trained professionals. Expecting parents, teachers and other caretakers **to learn & do the work** of treatment professionals is unrealistic and unnecessary. Of course, it is desirable for the child's parents, caretakers, teachers and others to **collaborate** with the treatment providers. If they're not collaborating with the treatment providers, legitimate treatment is not being delivered. However, if the "naturally occurring resources" in the child's life are not willing or able to take up the hard work that is necessary to teach the child necessary new skills, how can that be a justification for not teaching those skills to the child? Obviously, it isn't.

Titration Planning

Funding agencies seek to reduce or eliminate treatment funding. That is the primary reason for their existence. One of their favorite tactics is the "titration plan." This is usually marketed as a scheme where a soothsayer with a license to practice a profession channels Nostradamus and makes predictions (without any evidence *whatsoever* to support their prognostications), about the future needs of the patient. In the children's mental health treatment field, the soothsayer often divines that the child will need 25% fewer hours of treatment, usually "to reduce dependency on the staff" so that, by the end of the funding authorization period, the funding agency's expenses are cut by 25% or more. The overarching goal is to spread treatment funding as far and wide as possible, albeit an inch deep (like making toothpicks). Certificates of Excellence and commemorative plaques for politicians are awarded for such service to the community.

The staff of the Institute for Behavior Change approach titration very differently. While they are reducing or eliminating unnecessary dependency on service providers, the method they use allows the child to receive precisely the amount of intensive, individualized treatment that he or she requires, as their troublesome behavior waxes and wanes, until the treatment plan is completed successfully. This method brings a healthy dose of *reality* into the treatment planning process.

When the child has the *inevitable* experience of frustration that exceeds his or her capacity for tolerance, and regression begins to occur, the treatment provider can judiciously come to the child's aid *because they are still part of the child's life.* An ethical treatment provider can **prevent** the catastrophe that occurs when the soothsayer's "titration" plan is followed and the child's treatment hours are cut by the magical ratio of 25%, then 50%, then 75% over the span of a few future months.

A TITRATION PLAN THAT MAKES SENSE

The Titration Plan is to "titrate" (reduce the intensity of) 1:1 intensive, individualized treatment (TSS support) provided to [child] as conscientiously as possible throughout the treatment period *without depriving [child] of necessary support, especially in emergencies.* The TSS provider will seek to decrease the level of prompting (move from direct and physical prompts to indirect and verbal or symbolic prompts) and will seek to increase the physical distance separating him/her from [child]. This will eliminate excessive dependency on the TSS provider and will assure that the TSS provider is available to [child] to deliver the least-restrictive and least-intrusive level of intervention necessary at any given time in the treatment period in accordance with CASSP Principles and BHRS Best Practice Guidelines. The level of prompting typically used with the child, and the TSS provider's typical distance from the child are recorded on the TSS Progress Note to facilitate evaluation of the progress and success of a Titration Plan that Makes Sense.

Titration that makes *Sense*

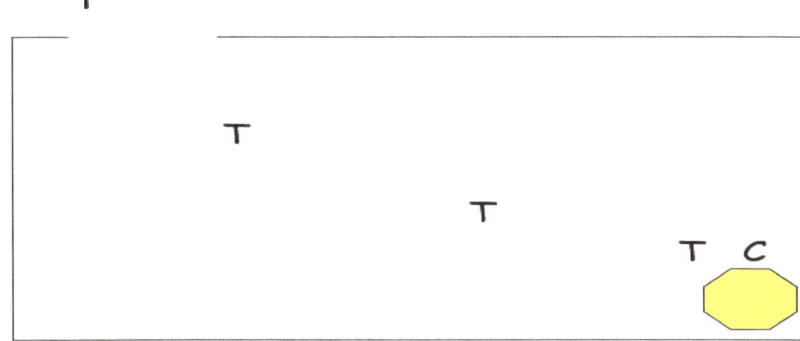

The treatment provider (T) works 20 or more hours per week with the child (C) while maintaining as much distance from the child as possible while delivering the treatment prompts, cues and other interventions necessary for learning and practice of new skills to take place. When the treatment provider has consistently been at maximum distance from the child for 2-4 weeks, it can safely be concluded that the termination of the treatment plan is justified. *Then,* the treatment provider begins to work with another child who needs 20 or more hours of treatment, and so on, and so on.

Crisis and Emergency Plan	An individualized crisis and emergency plan is needed for each child. Common elements will include notifying police in the event of elopement from assigned areas, serious injury or other such events. To the extent possible, these circumstances should be anticipated so that a plan for responding to them is in place before they occur. Notification of funding agencies should be addressed here so that no allegations of negligence are forthcoming after the crisis has been managed. Contacting 911 should be included so that it is always clear that treatment service providers are not *caretakers*.
Titration Plan	The Titration Plan is to "titrate" (reduce the intensity of) TSS support provided to [child] as conscientiously as possible throughout the treatment period *without depriving [child] of necessary support, especially in emergencies.* The TSS provider will seek to decrease the level of prompting (move from direct and physical prompts to indirect and verbal or symbolic prompts) and will seek to increase the physical distance separating him/her from [child]. This will eliminate excessive dependency on the TSS provider and will assure that the TSS provider is available to [child] to deliver the least-restrictive and least-intrusive level of intervention necessary at any given time in the treatment period in accordance with CASSP Principles and BHRS Best Practice Guidelines. The level of prompting typically used with [child], and the TSS provider's typical distance from the child will be recorded on the TSS Progress Note to facilitate evaluation of the progress and success of the Titration Plan.
Transition Plan	Over the course of his/her treatment program, [child] will be redirected to as many community-based providers of low-cost or no-cost alternatives to professional mental health service providers as possible, so that all potential replacements for Behavioral Health Rehabilitation Service (BHRS) providers will be achieved as quickly and conscientiously as possible, so long as the quality and quantity of BHRS is never reduced below the level necessary to reasonably achieve the goal of reducing, eliminating or preventing the worsening of the target behavior identified in his/her BHRS treatment plan. Potential providers of such alternatives include, but are not limited to: Religious organizations (whether or not he/she is a member of a given congregation, [child] may be allowed to participate in youth group programs at any of several community churches or other places of worship and the possibility of such participation should be explored vigorously), The BHRS Team will review the progress of this Transition Plan via a review of the CASSP Principles at each ISPT meeting.
Discharge Plan	The average of parent ratings of [child]'s involvement in target behavior over the past four weeks is reported in the chart below. A score of 2 or lower is within normal limits for a typically-developing child of the same age. A score above 2 indicates abnormal behavior that requires professional intervention. The highest possible score is 10. The higher the score, the more *intensively* and *urgently* this professional intervention is needed. The Plan is to discontinue BHR Services in the least amount of time possible in which to enable [child] to attain and generalize behavioral goals, which is defined as the time when the average of parent frequency and severity ratings of the target behavior reaches the Discharge Criteria. Over the past four weeks, the average distance between the TSS provider and the client was [insert] feet and the highest level of prompting used was [insert].

Target behavior	Discharge Criteria	Average for last four weeks
target1	*cutoff1* for four consecutive weeks	
target2	*cutoff2* for four consecutive weeks	
target3	*cutoff3* for four consecutive weeks	

What is a Likert Scale?

A Likert (*LIK-ərt*) scale is a psychometric scale that is frequently used in questionnaires and is mistakenly confused with the term *rating scale.* Psychologist Rensis Likert created the scale in 1932, emphasizing that responses are scored along a *range.* Respondents typically indicate their level of agreement or disagreement on a symmetric scale (equal numbers of "negative" options and "positive options" exist on either side of a median "neutral" option). In this way, a Likert scale is used to document the degree of endorsement along the continuum of opinions. In common practice, five response levels are used. Most Likert scales contain *odd* numbers of items (the middle always being a "neutral" option) but a "forced choice" model also exists which is intended to deter respondents from always choosing the most noncommittal option.

Comparison of Likert Scales and the Kossor Scale: Sources of error

Likert scales are subject to distortion from several causes, especially a "**central tendency**" bias (choosing the middle option which is usually the most noncommittal choice). Another source of bias occurs when repeated questions are asked about the same subject – respondents tend to become more emphatic over time as a means of "making their voice heard." None of these biases can be corrected through statistical normalization methods.

The Kossor Scale minimizes the central tendency bias. It minimizes social desirability bias by providing specific criteria for the rating at each of the 10 points along the continua of each scale, and by engaging the rater and the treatment provider in a dialogue, reflecting on past ratings. As a result, a progressively clearer and more nuanced understanding of the child's behavior and responses to the treatment plan is obtained by the rater and by the clinicians providing and supervising treatment. Likert scales also are prone to distortion because most people will agree with statements as presented. This is called an "**acquiescence**" bias. This bias is most often seen in respondents who are young, developmentally delayed, elderly or otherwise diminished in their capacity to assert themselves (possibly the result of cultural or institutional experiences).

The Kossor Scale minimizes acquiescence bias because the treatment provider behaves ethically and does not coerce the rater to acquiesce to preconceived beliefs or expectations. In any case, when the rater's evaluation differs significantly from those of the other treatment providers, the discrepancy is obvious, reported and discussed so that the rater acquires a more thorough and complete understanding of the child's behavior.

Respondents to Likert scales often display a "**social desirability**" bias. They respond defensively to avoid confrontation. They provide answers that they believe will be evaluated favorably by authorities ("faking good") or answers that they believe will be evaluated negatively by authorities ("faking bad"). Almost all users of Likert scales explicitly eschew *any* interaction between the rater and the examiner out of fear that the examiner might unduly influence the respondent.

When irreconcilable differences between a parent's ratings and the treatment provider's ratings occur, it is important for those differences to be reconciled in order for treatment to proceed. Collaboration does not exist in the presence of irreconcilable differences, and responsible, ethical treatment cannot be delivered without collaboration between caregivers and treatment providers.

Accordingly, the documentation of noncollaboration is unequivocally established if it occurs, and the termination of ineffective or otherwise inappropriate treatment can be expedited. This is a particularly valuable rationale for using the Kossor Scale for treatment outcome measurement.

The Kossor Scale facilitates **understanding** on the part of the rater that the ratings cannot be used as a means of manipulatively causing treatment to persist when it is not working or needed. A parent who persistently rates the child's frequency or severity of target behavior very highly (when other evaluators persistently rate those variables much lower) can be confronted with the disparity between their ratings and the others' ratings.

Noncollaboration is obvious when the parent persists in rating the child's behavior inaccurately. When ratings have no variance (the rating is "10" week after week), some ulterior motive probably lies at the root of the ratings being given (or a nonliving entity is being monitored). When such fallacious uses of the Kossor Scale become apparent, the treatment provider might legitimately ask if it is permissible to deliver treatment in a corrupt system that is probably incapable of benefitting from it.

Likert scales are arbitrary, the Kossor Scale is not

The value assigned to a Likert item has no objective numerical basis. The value assigned to each item in a Kossor Scale is explicitly defined. The value assigned to each Likert item is an arbitrary point on a continuum or range of general options. The value assigned to each Kossor Scale item is explicitly defined as a point on a continuum or range of mental health and illness symptoms that do not overlap adjacent levels.

Likert scales typically range from 2 to 10 – with 5 or 7 being the most common. Kossor Scales are always 10 items with no "safe midpoint" to offer a convenient default answer to the rater. Unlike Likert scales, where each successive item is treated as indicating a 'better' response than the preceding value, each successive item in a Kossor Scale is treated as indicating a "worse" response than the preceding value. The Kossor Scale is measuring *aberrant* "target" behavior that is explicitly defined operationally, not "improvement" which is much more difficult to operationally define and is therefore more prone to error. It is much easier to define aberrant target behavior in binary terms – it is either present or absent – and its measurement is less prone to error.

The Kossor Scale is *demonstrably* objective. The rating responses are explicitly defined through **dialogue** between the examiner and the rater for each case that is being monitored and this dialogue occurs **each time** ratings are obtained. The possibility of interpretive error is eliminated in the Kossor Scale, as long as the rater and the examiner engage in this dialogue in the process of data collection. By assessing treatment outcome in terms of the reduction of *aberrant* (target) behavior, it is much harder to declare a treatment program "successful" if *quality of life* has not improved. Reducing aberrant (target) behavior must be accompanied by increasing adaptive (replacement) behavior and the Kossor Scale, with its emphasis on dialogue, facilitates this. Most importantly from a statistical analysis perspective, the Kossor Scale is unequivocally an **interval** scale; the 'distance' between items is defined explicitly in symmetric and equidistant terms. No rating could simultaneously be given to more than one point on the Kossor Scale and the role of the treatment supervisor is to enable the rater to understand this basic concept.

Responses to the Kossor Scale rarely show a normal or quasi-normal distribution because the scale is measuring *aberrant* behavior. Aberrant behavior never occurs in a normal distribution; it peaks during certain conditions and ebbs during other conditions. It is maintained or suppressed by the **skill set** of the person who displays it, not simply by the consequences that follow it. By tracking the incidence and intensity (frequency and severity) of aberrant behavior that has been explicitly defined in binary terms, it is possible to track the occurrence of that behavior with a high degree of accuracy. When aberrant behavior ebbs, adaptive behavior can emerge (and it will do so, if it is rewarded – reinforced – in accordance with the basic principles of behavior analysis).

Responses on the Kossor Scale may be summed because the scale is an interval scale, so the central limit theorem allows treatment of the data as interval data measuring a latent variable. Because the summed or average responses fulfill these assumptions, parametric statistical tests such as the analysis of variance can be applied. The literature commonly cites a minimum of 4 and preferably 8 items in the sum. Scores from at least 10 (and up to 13) items from the Kossor Scale for over 1,000 treatment programs have been analyzed in studies of treatment outcomes conducted by independent researchers from four different educational institutions since 2007. Non-parametric tests such as chi-squared test, Mann–Whitney test, Wilcoxon signed-rank test, or Kruskal–Wallis test can be used in the analysis of Likert scale or Kossor Scale data.

Frequency scores and Severity scores can be studied separately, or the average ratings in a baseline period can be compared with the average of ratings in the final four weeks of any treatment period. As with Likert scale data, Kossor Scale data can be analyzed via Consensus Based Assessment (CBA) to create an objective standard in domains where no generally accepted or objective standard exists. Consensus based assessment can be used to refine or validate generally accepted standards. In addition, Hierarchical Linear Modeling (HLM) has been used with a large database of Kossor Scale data and yielded highly significant ($p < .001$) findings of a powerful association between treatment exposure and aberrant behavior reduction. That's an error estimate of *less than one in ten thousand.*

Whether individual Likert items can be considered as interval-level data, or whether they should be treated as ordered-categorical data has been the subject of considerable disagreement in the literature, with strong convictions on both sides. This disagreement can be traced back to the extent to which Likert items were interpreted as being ordinal data. Research by Labovitz (1967) and Traylor (1983) provide evidence that, even with rather large distortions of perceived distances between scale points, Likert-type items perform closely to scales that are perceived as equal intervals. Therefore, both Likert Scale and Kossor Scale items meet the standards many researchers believe are required for parametric statistical procedures and tests.

Validity refers to how well a tool measures what it intends to measure. Criterion-referenced measures like the Kossor Scale tend to have the highest levels of validity. With each rater using the same tool to measure an outcome repeatedly, it is possible to evaluate the reliability of the measure. Since the rater and the treatment provider collaborate in obtaining the rating each week when using the Kossor Scale, the consistency of the rater's evaluation actually *increases* over time, thereby raising the reliability of the measure to the point that it approaches 1.0 within a typical 18 week evaluation period.

The rate of increase in reliability is rapid, so that ratings within a 10-week period can be considered highly reliable if the rating has been obtained in a dialogue between the treatment recipient and the supervisor of the treatment program.

Establishing validity requires establishing both reliability and accuracy (i.e., that the ratings represent what they are supposed to represent). The degree of validity of an instrument is determined through the application of logic/or statistical procedures. Since the Kossor Scale is a criterion-referenced measure that is individualized to the particular treatment plan being monitored, it necessarily has extremely high content, predictive and construct validity and high reliability as well if it is used with fidelity. The widespread belief that it is impossible to evaluate the reliability or validity of user ratings may be due to the primitive nature of user rating scales that were developed for advertising campaigns and other pseudoscientific applications of statistical principles over the decades. The Kossor Scale might be considered an evolutionary enhancement of the Likert scale.

Recent Studies – 2013 and 2016

Investigations were undertaken in 2013 and 2016 to evaluate the utility of the *Effective Treatment in a Wraparound Cup®* model ("the ET model of BHRS") by examining its efficacy in treating a specific population: children and adolescents under the age of 18 diagnosed with an Autism Spectrum Disorder (ASD).

The following two studies examined the efficacy of this BHRS treatment model that combines the practices and principles of two widely recognized evidence based practices ("Applied Behavior Analysis" and "Full Fidelity Wraparound") to deliver Behavior Specialist Consultant (BSC), Mobile Therapy (MT), and Therapeutic Staff Support (TSS) services to children with ASD, using traditional behavior modification practices (prompting, fading, shaping, etc.). The studies hypothesized that treatment rendered to children with ASD utilizing the ET model of BHRS would ameliorate symptoms of their behavioral health diagnosis across five treatment domains, namely physical aggression, lack of safety awareness, socialization deficits, communication deficits and non-compliance. Furthermore, it was hypothesized that there would be a significant reduction in target aberrant behavior frequency, severity and duration from baseline to the ending weeks of treatment, across demographic variables (race, gender, income level).

Participants

A sample of 82 children who met criteria for a diagnosis on the autism spectrum (as outlined in the *Diagnostic and Statistical Manual of Mental Disorders, Fourth and Fifth Editions)* were enrolled in BHRS during the given data collection period. Their participation and consent was determined through the initial authorization to provide treatment signed by the child's parent/guardian, if the child was under the age of 14 or declared mentally incompetent, at the time of the initial behavioral intake and evaluation. If the child was age 14 or older, treatment and subsequent participation in data collection was authorized also with the consent of the child. All necessary demographic information was collected and behavioral goal domains were selected prior to the start of treatment, typically identified by a BSC using an Information Questionnaire for a Life Domain Bio-Psycho-Social Evaluation (modeled after the recommendations of Gordon Hodas, Pennsylvania Department of Public Welfare, 2001). All subjects were either past or current clients of the Network for Behavior Change, a private psychology practice in Southeastern Pennsylvania.

Measures

The primary research materials utilized in these studies were two forms filled out and updated by treatment team members throughout the child's treatment period. First, demographic information was collected by a BSC using an initial referral and intake form. A parent/guardian of each child reported information based on the child's sex, race, age, household income level, and initial reports of areas of behavioral symptoms.

In order to determine behavioral measures and outcomes with respect to each child's individualized treatment plan, a *Parent Report of Progress (PRP)* was used which incorporated the Kossor Scale. The PRP had the dual purpose of recording and tracking client behavioral data weekly while creating an opportunity for weekly dialogue between treatment providers and the parents/caregivers of children receiving treatment so that a reliable and valid measurement of treatment progress could be obtained from the parent of the child receiving treatment. Containing up to thirteen weeks of data collection, the PRP was designed to obtain weekly ratings from the child's parent/caregiver. The Kossor Scale was used to record the frequency and severity of the child's presentation of target behavior for each of their three current treatment domains (drawn from five possible domains: physical aggression, communication, socialization, non-compliance, and safety awareness).

Prior to enrollment in treatment, the empirically validated Childhood Autism Rating Scale – second edition (CARS-2) was also administered to facilitate the diagnosis of ASD (Garfin, McCallon & Cox, 1988). This measure was also repeated at approximately quarterly intervals (as a part of the BHRS reauthorization process) with the final measure taken within three months or less prior to discharge in most cases. TSS treatment providers also completed daily encounter forms ("Progress Notes") documenting the child's behavior and their interface with the child, and these were compared with PRP responses to maximize the reliability and validity of both staff encounter data and PRP data. When discrepancies were noted, these were discussed with both parties in order to improve their understanding of behavioral treatment components and expectations.

Procedure

Subjects were introduced to the provider organization when a parent/guardian initiated contact via a Referral Form, seeking treatment for behavioral issues associated with their child's referral diagnosis of ASD. After a brief phone screening where Medicaid eligibility was determined, a BSC was assigned to conduct an intake assessment. If BHRS was indicated, subjects were evaluated by a licensed psychologist who conducted a Life-Domain Bio-Psycho-Social evaluation.

Input from the BSC, the child's parent (and the child's teacher if BHRS appeared to be necessary in the school), was sought, measuring the subject's strengths, weaknesses and needs in accordance with standards established by the Pennsylvania Department of Public Welfare (Gordon Hodas, Pennsylvania Department of Public Welfare, 2001).

Immediately following the completion of the child's evaluation, the parents/guardians, licensed psychologist, and BSC assigned to the case met to finalize an initial treatment plan and to assure parental understanding and intent to collaborate with the BHRS process.

A BHRS description form was presented to the parents of the child for their review and approval prior to the implementation of BHRS; if the child was age 14 or older, the child's consent was similarly obtained. Each child's treatment plan consisted of operationally defined target behaviors and operationally defined replacement behaviors paired with explicitly defined intervention methods (specifying the exact procedure to be used, by whom, when, and where). A Crisis Intervention Plan, Transition Plan (to replace BHRS with low-cost or no-cost alternatives), Titration Plan (to reduce or eliminate Bachelors-level TSS service if it was prescribed) and a Discharge Plan were developed before treatment commenced.

Treatment plans incorporated the principles of ABA, Full Fidelity Wraparound, elements of the Floortime approach, Discrete Trial Training (Dillenburger and Keenan, 2009; Lovaas, 1987; Pajareya and Nopmaneejumruslers, 2011; Strain and Schwartz, 2001; Tsiouri et al., 2012), Intensive Behavioral Treatment (Kossor, 1999), Evidence Based Kernels (Embry and Biglan, 2008) and other interventions as determined to be necessary by the licensed psychologist. Three behavioral domains were identified for intervention, chosen from five potential domains: physical aggression, lack of environmental safety, noncompliance with adult prompts, communication deficits and socialization deficits, in an initial projected treatment period of four months.

Each subject received an individually prescribed combination of BSC, MT and TSS services, delivered weekly as prescribed for a varying number of hours. The BSC met with the family (and school officials if necessary) on a weekly basis to monitor treatment progress and MT and/or TSS service delivery. During their weekly meeting, the BSC engaged the subject's parent/guardian in a consultation, during which the PRP was administered, in person or via telephone. The operational definition of the child's target behavior was discussed with the parent. For example, the "physical aggression" target behavior domain might be operationally defined as "hitting, kicking and spitting" for an individual child. The parent was then asked to rate the frequency, for the given calendar week, of the child's engagement in "hitting, kicking and spitting" on an annotated Likert scale from 1 to 10, using defined benchmarks that facilitate rapid and accurate assessment on a continuum where 10 is a "constant" frequency of the target behavior. A rating of "2" is considered the upper limit of acceptable for a child of the same age.

Likewise, a measurement of the Severity of the behavior was taken. This process was then repeated for the operational definitions of each subject's two other treatment domains. Once the parent supplied frequency and severity data for a given domain, the BSC computed an arithmetic mean for the Frequency and Severity of each target behavior domain, serving as the final weekly treatment outcome measure in that domain.

Likewise, a measure for the other two behavioral domains was calculated. This process was repeated by the BSC for each week of the child's prescribed treatment period despite any lapse in the face-to-face delivery of BSC, MT and/or TSS service delivery, assessing the same set of behaviors until revised by the Treatment Team with the consent of the licensed psychologist. Treatment was discontinued if/when the subject met discharge criteria (the pre-determined rating on the PRP for four consecutive weeks) or if the child's caretakers were not collaborating sufficiently with the BHRS providers over a period of at least four consecutive weeks. If BHRS was determined to be an inadequate level of care to meet the needs of the child, a referral to a higher level of care was made to the Treatment Team by the licensed psychologist.

Analysis

A series of paired sample t-tests were conducted to compare the averages of frequency and severity data, utilizing baseline and outcome means obtained through the Parent Report of Progress (PRP). Baseline means were the average ratings for the first four weeks of a given treatment period. Outcome means were the average of the last four consecutive recorded ratings on the PRP in each behavioral domain.

The subjects' baseline and outcome means for each individual treatment goal domain were paired to establish a set of repeated measures, analyzing at least 10 and up to 13 weeks of data collected. Data collected was sorted and split by reported demographic variables (gender, race, income level) as well as by behavioral domain (physical aggression, communication, socialization, safety awareness, non-compliance). Paired-sample t-tests were conducted on the entire sample and each individual group to determine any possible between-subject effects.

In Study #1, subjects' scores were not always from the last four weeks of treatment or post-treatment due to episodic data collection failures. As with baseline scores, subjects whose data did not reflect completed treatment were included. In Study #2, subjects with less than 10 weeks of treatment outcome data were excluded, resulting in a smaller sample size.

Results – Study #1 (2013)

Two hundred forty six treatment plans from 78 children were analyzed (mean of 3.15 plans per subject across the treatment duration); 64 (26%) addressed communication deficits, 61 (24.8%) addressed socialization deficits, 60 (24.4%) addressed noncompliance with adult prompts, 38 (15.4%) addressed a lack of safety awareness, and 23 (9.3%) addressed physical aggression. Treatment duration ranged from 4-450 weeks (mean 80.41 weeks), with 85.5% of treatments lasting less than 3 years.

Analysis revealed an improvement from baseline to outcome measurements across the full sample, $t(245) = 5.366$, $p < .001$. Analysis of cases from each treatment goal found a statistically significant improvement in treatments addressing physical aggression ($t(22) = 4.159$, $p < .001$), socialization deficits ($t(60) = 2.485$, $p = .016$), and a lack of safety awareness ($t(37) = 3.964$, $p < .001$).

No significant improvements in behavior were found for treatment plans addressing noncompliance with adult prompts ($t(59) = 1.366$, $p = .177$) or communication deficits ($t(63) = 1.303$, $p = .197$). Further analyses were conducted examining the effect of treatment on various demographic groups. Significant improvement was found in treatments of children of Caucasian ($t(161) = 3.655$, $p < .001$) and Asian descent ($t(32) = 5.086$, $p < .001$). No significant change was found for African American ($t(32) = 1.110$, $p = .275$) or Hispanic ($t(17) = 1.271$, $p = .221$) children.

A significant improvement was found when treating males ($t(220) = 5.288$, $p < .001$) but not females ($t(24) = 1.385$, $p = .179$). Significant differences between baseline and outcome were noted for subjects living above ($t(44) = 2.096$, $p = .042$) and below ($t(197) = 5.158$, $p < .001$) the federal poverty level.

Discussion – Study #1

The results indicate that the ET model of BHRS that included TSS attenuated behavioral symptoms in most, but not all populations of children and adolescents with ASD. Importantly, it should be noted that many children were referred to BHRS treatment because of worsening behavior. Frequently, stabilization, and not just improvement, is considered a successful treatment outcome.

In fact, the initial treatment plan specifies a designated amount of time where, if behavior remains stable, treatment will cease. The finding that BHRS treatment via the ET model caused a significant decrease in behavioral issues despite this nuance further strengthens the findings in this study. While results were positive, analyses revealed that the ET model of BHRS was not as effective in attenuating behavioral issues in females or individuals of African American and Hispanic descent. Further investigations are needed to elucidate why not all children gained comparable benefits. While staff at the Institute for Behavior Change received cultural competency education as a facet of their initial training, more rigorous matching of TSS providers' personality and other attributes with assigned children may improve the consistency of positive treatment outcomes.

Since none of the treatment populations experienced a significant increase in behavioral issues, it can be concluded that the ET model of BHRS served to stop behavioral deterioration in all groups.

Results – Study #2 (2016)

One hundred sixty five treatment plans from 55 children were analyzed (mean of 3.0 plans per subject across treatment duration). Subjects ranged in age from 3-18 years (M=8.6), composed of Caucasian (66%), Black (11%), Hispanic (7%), Asian (16%) respondents, with self-reports of income level indicating those below (76%) and above (24%) the Federal Poverty Level. Physical aggression (8%), communication deficits (27%), socialization deficits (14%), non-compliance with adult prompts (27%), and socialization deficits (24%) were targeted behavior.

Analyses were conducted examining the effect of treatment on various demographic groups. With respect to race, there was a significance difference between baseline (M = 6.28, SD = 1.73) and outcome (M = 4.85, SD = 1.19) means for Asian subjects; $t(26) = -4.79$, $p<.001$ as well as a significant difference between baseline (M = 6.23, SD = 1.82) and outcome (M = 6.86, SD = 1.81) means for Black subjects; $t(17) = 2.21$, $p = 0.041$. There was no significant difference in baseline and outcome PRP measures for Caucasian ($p = .062$) or Hispanic ($p = .913$) subjects.

A significant difference was found between baseline (M = 5.99, SD = 1.59) and outcome (M = 5.54, SD = 1.54) means for male subjects; $t(149) = -4.06$, $p<.001$ and for subjects living in households reporting income levels below the poverty line; $t(125) = -3.60$, $p<.001$. There were no differences between PRP measures for female subjects ($p = .060$) or those with reported household incomes above the poverty level ($p = .204$). There was no significant difference between baseline and outcomes means for any of the five individual treatment plan behavioral domains. Yet, a significant difference was determined between baseline (M = 5.97, SD = 1.60) and outcome (M = 5.65, SD = 1.58) means for the collective sample of subjects; $t(164) = -2.75$, $p = 0.007$

Discussion – Study #2

Due to the inherent subjective and individual nature of BHR services and treatment, based on the specific treatment needs of an individual, it is difficult to develop a comprehensive study to determine the efficacy of a given treatment model. Yet with the use of criterion-referenced tools such as the Parent Report of Progress (PRP), acting as a dual quality of life assessment and behavioral progress determinant, the effects of the ET model of BHRS on ameliorating the symptoms of ASD diagnoses in children can be easily analyzed.

For several demographic variables, the results indicated that the ET model of BHRS treatment composed of a prescribed combination of BSC, MT, and TSS services significantly attenuated behavioral symptoms. Due to the relatively large number of males diagnosed with ASD compared to female counterparts, it is unsurprising that a significant decrease in target behavior was found for male subjects. This effect would likely be replicated for females with ASD in a sample with a larger number of female subjects participating in treatment.

With respect to income, it is also unsurprising that the largest group represented in the sample, those with household income levels below the Federal Poverty Level, revealed a significant difference in baseline and outcome means, suggesting a decrease in behavioral symptoms over the treatment period.

When examining effects between racial groups, a significant decrease in symptoms was determined in Asian subjects, with a significant increase in behavioral symptoms over the treatment period for Black subjects, and no significant difference for the other groups. Again, these findings are likely to due to the small sample size and lack of significant racial diversity in the makeup of our participant group.

It should be noted that although cultural competency is a facet of the ET model and training, there is always room for improvement in this particular area of development and practice, creating a culturally diverse and astute staff of treatment providers to reflect the makeup of the client population.

Overall, the composite analysis of the sample's baseline and outcome means revealed a significant decrease in symptoms for subjects with ASD across demographic variables and treatment plan domains, despite no significant difference occurring between individual behavioral domains. This is the most important indicator of the efficacy and applicability of the ET model of BHRS to larger, more diverse populations of children with ASD requiring treatment for behavioral concerns. A study with a larger sample is in progress. It was expected that this study would result in a definitive positive reflection on the ability of the ET model to ameliorate aberrant behavior in children with ASD. Evidence supporting this hypothesis was found in Study #1.

Importantly, as was noted in Study #1, many children were referred to BHRS treatment because of worsening behavior. Accordingly, stabilization, and not just improvement, is a successful treatment outcome. In fact, the initial treatment plan specifies a designated amount of time where, if behavior remains stable, treatment will cease. Thus, any finding that BHRS treatment caused a significant decrease in behavioral issues despite this nuance further strengthens the findings in the two present studies.

Limitations

While these studies provided additional evidence of the efficacy of the ET model of BHRS, there were a number of limitations. It should be noted that there are inherent limitations in examining BHRS treatment in any scientific evaluation; because BHRS is individualized to the needs of the child, each treatment uses different interventions and requires varied amounts of treatment hours per week. Due to this, caution must be taken in generalizing these results, as the makeup of BHRS treatment varies widely between providers, and even more so for individual cases. This examination can only claim to provide evidence for the efficacy of the ET model of BHRS treatment that integrates ABA practices and Full Fidelity Wraparound principles under the supervision of a licensed psychologist, with the treatment quantity and quality determined on an individual basis for each recipient.

The primary limitation for the present two studies was the lack of a control group. As data collection was a portion of an ongoing professional mental health practice, it was not ethically permissible to withhold treatment from subjects enrolled in treatment. Further study of the ET model would benefit from a repeated measures design highlighting the effects of periods during which services lapsed or when gaps in service delivery occurred due to staff illness or other factors, to determine the persistence of treatment progress following lapses in treatment delivery. The Kossor Scale for treatment outcome measurement was used in the Parent Report of Progress (PRP). It was chosen due to its criterion-referenced nature and ease of administration and clarity for parents. Clinical practice necessitated that parents assess the child's progress on a weekly basis.

Yet several issues exist with the reliability of the PRP due to the nature of its structure and subjectivity of respondents. Parents could conceivably have an expectancy bias in their ratings, perceiving behavior improvements due to the presence of treatment, or may report that their child is not improving as a means of coercing the extension of treatment inappropriately and unnecessarily. However, since BHRS cannot be delivered "for the convenience of parents or staff," it is unlikely that parents would be allowed to manipulate the data collection process except for infrequent discrete violations by particular individuals. The repeated collection of high ratings for behavioral frequency and severity would indicate the failure of the BHRS program, and necessitate its replacement by a more intensive level of treatment, for example.

Although parents are expected to be "in charge" of their child's education according to the Federal Education Rights and Privacy Act (FERPA), they may not be a sufficiently knowledgeable rater for the frequency and severity of behavior occurring in school or community settings, unless they can rely on the reports received from teachers, BHRS providers and others. The consistency with which such reports are given to parents by teachers and other school authorities, and their depth, has been diminishing consistently, especially over the past 20 years. Accordingly, weekly consultation between the BSC and the parent for delivering accurate information about behavioral observations in school that could facilitate accurate Parental Report of Progress is a prerequisite for accurate BHRS treatment outcome monitoring. Lastly, although a series of demographic variables were examined in the two present studies, they are likely not the best indicators in determining the efficacy of this treatment program. Within the data collection process of the second study, the length of the treatment program and the number of hours of service rendered within a given period were omitted.

In the first study, this information was included but was not referenced in the analysis that was submitted. Both of these factors should be included in further studies of BHRS models to determine the efficacy of treatment based on quantifiable measures of service delivery. Qualitative variables were omitted from both studies, with factors that may have played a large role in their child's progress giving no context to the PRP measure (e.g., child was ill, parents experiencing divorce, etc.)

Conclusions

Despite these limitations, the results are a promising step in examining the efficacy of the ET model of BHRS treatment for children with ASD. Further research is necessary to examine BHRS treatment to examine factors that improve treatment outcomes across all behavioral domains.

Use of the PAX Good Behavior Game in school classrooms is an example. For BHRS to be optimally successful in varying settings and with varying populations of children, some essential components are recommended, especially for the treatment of children with Autism Spectrum Disorders:

1. The BHRS program should include Therapeutic Staff Support (TSS) services in an amount, duration and scope that is consistent with published standards by the National Academy of Sciences (2001) and the American Academy of Pediatrics (2007, 2012) for children with Autism Spectrum Disorders (a minimum of 25 hours of "intensive, individualized treatment" per week, year-round).

2. TSS services should be provided by Bachelors level mental health professionals who receive ongoing training and supervision by licensed mental health professionals and Masters level mental health professionals regarding the use of evidence-based practices including "evidence-based kernels," ABA practices and Full Fidelity Wraparound principles in the therapeutic management and redirection of aberrant behavior in children.

3. The treatment planning and delivery process should be overseen by licensed mental health professionals (especially licensed psychologists with expertise in treating children) who devote at least one hour weekly to the supervision of the Masters-level Behavior Specialist providers, who in turn provide individual weekly supervision to the TSS providers.

4. The treatment plan should be a written document that includes operationally defined target and replacement behavior (such that the behavior can be measured unequivocally by the TSS provider and the parent or other caregivers), explicitly defined implementation methodology and unequivocal crisis intervention, titration, transition and discharge plans.

5. The progress of the child in treatment should be monitored weekly by the parent in a collaborative process wherein the Behavior Specialist assists the parent in making an informed assessment of the frequency and severity of the child's target (aberrant) behavior in the past week by comparing it to the behavior displayed in the preceding week.

REFERENCES

Armstrong, Robert (1987). "The midpoint on a Five-Point Likert-Type Scale." *Perceptual and Motor Skills.* **64** (2): 359–362. *doi*:10.2466/pms.1987.64.2.359.

B Robbins, Naomi; M Heiberger, Richard (2011). "Plotting Likert and Other Rating Scales." *JSM 2011: 1058–1066.*

Babbie, Earl R. (2005). *The Basics of Social Research.* Belmont, CA: Thomson Wadsworth. p. 174. *ISBN 0-534-63036-7.*

Baer, D.M.; Wolf, M.M.; Risley, T.R. (1968). "Some current dimensions of applied behavior analysis." *Journal of Applied Behavior Analysis* **1** (1): 91–97. doi:10.1901/jaba.1968.1-91. PMC 1310980. PMID 16795165.

Burns, Alvin; Burns, Ronald (2008). *Basic Marketing Research (Second ed.).* New Jersey: Pearson Education. p. 245. *ISBN 978-0-13-205958-9.*

Carifio, James; Perla, Rocco J. (2007). "Ten Common Misunderstandings, Misconceptions, Persistent Myths and Urban Legends about Likert Scales and Likert Response Formats and their Antidotes." *Journal of Social Sciences.* **3** (3): 106–116. *doi*:10.3844/jssp.2007.106.116.

Dawes, John (2008). "Do Data Characteristics Change According to the number of scale points used? An experiment using 5-point, 7-point and 10-point scales." *International Journal of Market Research.* **50** (1): 61–77.

Heward W.L. (2005) Reasons applied behavior analysis is good for education and why those reasons have been insufficient. In: Heward W. L, et al., editors. Focus on behavior analysis in education: Achievements challenges, and opportunities. Upper Saddle River, NJ: Pearson Education, Inc.; 2005. pp. 318–348.

Jamieson, Susan (2004). "Likert Scales: How to (Ab)use Them." Medical Education, Vol. 38(12), pp. 1217-1218.

Johanson, George A.; Gips, Crystal J. (1993). "Paired Comparison Intransitivity: Useful Information or Nuisance?" (PDF). Paper presented at the Annual Meeting of the American Educational Research Association (Atlanta, GA, April 12–16, 1993).

Kossor, S (2016). The Issachar Project NSP Press.

Labovitz, S (1967). "Some observations on measurement and statistics." Social Forces. **46**: 151–160. doi:10.2307/2574595.

Latham, Gary P. (2006). *Work Motivation: History, Theory, Research, And Practice.* Thousand Oaks, Calif.: Sage Publications. p. 15. *ISBN 0-7619-2018-8.*

Likert, Rensis (1932). "A Technique for the Measurement of Attitudes." *Archives of Psychology.* **140**: 1–55.

Meyers, Lawrence S.; Anthony Guarino; Glenn Gamst (2005). Applied Multivariate Research: Design and Interpretation. Sage Publications. p. 20. ISBN 1-4129-0412-9.

Mogey, Nora (March 25, 1999). "So You Want to Use a Likert Scale?" *Learning Technology Dissemination Initiative. Heriot-Watt University.*

Myers S. M. and Johnson C. P. (2007). Management of children with autism spectrum disorders. *Pediatrics 120: 2007-2362. DOI: 10.1542/peds.2007-2362, American Academy of Pediatrics.*
http://pediatrics.aappublications.org/content/120/5/1162.long

National Academy of Sciences (2001). Educating Children with Autism. Committee on Educational Interventions for Children with Autism. Washington DC: National Academy Press. https://www.nap.edu/catalog/10017/educating-children-with-autism

Norman, Geoff (2010). "Likert scales, levels of measurement and the "laws" of statistics." Advances in Health Science Education. Vol 15(5) pp 625-632.

*Reips, Ulf-Dietrich; Funke, Frederik (2008). "Interval level measurement with visual analogue scales in Internet-based research: VAS Generator." Behavior Research Methods. **40** (3): 699–704.* doi:10.3758/BRM.40.3.699. PMID 18697664.

Rosenblatt, A. I. and Carbone, P. S. (Eds.) (2012). Autism Spectrum Disorders: What Every Parent Needs to Know, American Academy of Pediatrics.
https://www.amazon.com/Autism-Spectrum-Disorders-Every-Parent/dp/1581106513

*Traylor, Mark (October 1983). "Ordinal and interval scaling." Journal of the Market Research Society. **25** (4): 297–303.*

Trochim, William M. (October 20, 2006). "Likert Scaling." *Research Methods Knowledge Base, 2nd Edition.*

Uebersax, John S. (2006). "Likert Scales: Dispelling the Confusion."

*van Alphen, A.; Halfens, R.; Hasman, A.; Imbos, T. (1994). "Likert or Rasch? Nothing is more applicable than good theory." Journal of Advanced Nursing. **20**: 196–201.* doi:10.1046/j.1365-2648.1994.20010196.x.

Wuensch, Karl L. (October 4, 2005). "What is a Likert Scale? and How Do You Pronounce 'Likert?'" *East Carolina University.*

CONTACT

Steve Kossor (my last name is pronounced with a short "o" sound, as in "copper")

Please write to me at info@ibc-pa.org

Suggestions for a defense against claw-back of previously paid treatment funding

In August of 2009, the Pennsylvania Department of Public Welfare (DPW, now DHS) issued written instructions to all of the Behavioral Health Managed Care Organizations (BH-MCOs) overseeing Behavioral Health Rehabilitation Services (BHRS) in Pennsylvania. Those instructions told them to add the official definition of "medically necessary" treatment found in the PA Bulletin at 55 Pa. Code § 1101.21(a) into all of their BHRS Provider contracts. All of them did. Pennsylvania regulations governing EPSDT funding track the Federal standard in the Medicaid Act almost verbatim.   Every other State has its own standard for "medically necessary" treatment in their State. In Pennsylvania, the definition of "medically necessary" treatment is that *a service, item or treatment that IS medically necessary is one that:*

- *Prevents the worsening of the child's condition OR*
- *Treats the child's condition and improves it OR*
- *Enables the child to maintain his/her functioning at a level comparable to children of similar age.*

If BHRS is prescribed by a licensed practitioner of the healing arts for **all three** of these reasons), there is absolutely no doubt that the services prescribed are all "medically necessary" according to Pennsylvania law. This means that they should be delivered **and funded** by EPSDT for any **one** of the reasons in *italics* above. If a treatment provider can document that medically necessary services were delivered to enable the recipient to maintain his/her functioning at a level comparable to children of similar age, among other reasons, an extremely potent argument for the retention of funds paid to deliver those services has been advanced. Fortunately for their members, most Medicaid BH-MCOs create standards that are compatible with State laws, and reconsider appeals of their decisions judiciously.

If the treatment provider can show that in the cases reviewed in the claw-back audit, *these objectives were being achieved*, it becomes patently inappropriate for a BH-MCO to claw-back payments for treatment **that was legally delivered and was achieving its intended purpose.** It strengthens the appeal enormously if the appeal documentation meets **all** published expectations (DPW, DHS, BH-MCO) for recording progress in the delivery of treatment. This means that the appeal has to explain in detail how the documentation was created in each child's case so that it created "a complete and contemporaneous record of service delivery" sufficient to monitor and assess the progress of the Treatment Plan being implemented and to facilitate any necessary changes in the Plan. For example:

- The child's "target" (aberrant) behavior has to have been explicitly defined,
- the intervention methods to be implemented by the treatment provider must have been identified and recorded clearly,
- the child's response to treatment must have been measured by a variety of means (including
    - the provider's distance from the child,
    - the level of prompting needed to deliver the interventions,
    - the presence of others in the environment who observed and/or engaged with the child must have been documented and examples of common antecedents to target behavior and examples of client responses must have been noted,
- outcome data must have been collected from the parent **every week** and
- the data must have been used to implement a BHRS treatment plan in full accordance with all of the principles of Full-Fidelity Wraparound and Applied Behavior Analysis.

Sometimes you just can't win, and that's unfortunate, but you keep helping where you can

Although the BHRS treatment model described in this book far exceeds the standards met by most other providers, it is still subject to BH-MCO audit. Some Medicaid BH-MCOs are permitted by State Medicaid Agencies (SMA) to create and impose their own peculiar standards on the BHRS providers in their networks, as if these Medicaid BH-MCOs somehow operate outside of SMA control. It is well-settled law in Pennsylvania that "governmental powers cannot be delegated to private individuals or organizations." *See Heatherington v. McHale*, 329 A.2d 250, 253 (Pa. 1974). Without any express authority from the legislature granting private or quasi-governmental entities the power to implement rules or regulations with regard to the Public Welfare Code, rulemaking authority is reserved exclusively to agencies of the Commonwealth. *See* 2 Pa.C.S. § 201 ("An agency shall have the power to promulgate...reasonable regulations implementing the provisions of this title."); *Pa. Builders Ass'n v. Dep't of Labor & Indus.*, 4 A.3d 215, 221 (Pa. Commw. Ct. 2010). Thus, a quasi-governmental agency like a BH-MCO, without the express authority from the legislature, cannot create policies or procedures that supersede the authority of a state agency such as the Department of Public Welfare (Human Services). The legislature has never expressly granted any BH-MCO authority to implement rules or regulations regarding the provisions of the Public Welfare Code that pertain to standards for outpatient mental health services, including BHRS. Yet, some do it with alacrity.

There has never been a published policy, procedure, law or other governance that unequivocally prohibits a parent from granting consent for the implementation of their child's BHRS treatment plan by verbal means using a telephone to communicate that consent. Yet, a BH-MCO can claim that telephonic permission given by the parent is insufficient to document the delivery of consent for the treatment program. To obtain a countersignature on the treatment plan or consent to treatment, *in addition to* the legitimate authorization of the parent obtained telephonically, may be a good idea to forestall BH-MCO claw-back attempts, but requiring it is an inappropriate and excessive interpretation that contradicts Pennsylvania law, DPW/DHS policy and long-standing statewide procedure. If BH-MCO auditors were also to claim that time spent writing treatment plans or consulting over the telephone (time not spent "face-to-face") was somehow not billable, they would be incorrect. If they insisted that a child with an Autism spectrum disorder required a minimum of 3 to 4 hours of *face-to-face* contact *every week* with a *licensed* Behavior Specialist in order to allow the delivery of 15 or more hours of weekly TSS service, they would be incorrect. Such BH-MCO standards are widely repudiated; even some officials in the State Medicaid Agency express private disagreement with them, yet they persist in some BH-MCOs for reasons that remain obscure.

To claw-back funds disbursed for *successful* treatment that was unequivocally medically necessary for supercilious reasons ought to be indefensible. An appeal of such audit findings might contain numerous examples of egregious administrative over-reach by BH-MCO auditors and consist of 300 pages of evidence and commentary, but it could still fail. Completely, with no recourse except arbitration and the courts which are prohibitively costly.

Sadly, a provider may have no alternative to leaving that Medicaid BH-MCO provider network to prevent unsettling audit experiences like these, while continuing to deliver its much-appreciated, effective BHRS treatment everywhere else. Increasing numbers of children are afflicted by disabilities whose symptoms can be alleviated significantly by the delivery of "medically necessary" treatment funded by the Medicaid EPSDT mandate. Medicaid BH-MCOs shouldn't be able to co-opt the *expressed, written purposes* of that mandate that were written into the laws of every US State since 1989, and deny **their** members help that members of **other** Medicaid BH-MCOs – including those in the very same State – can *routinely* receive.

The reader is referred to The Issachar Project (Kossor, 2016) for extensive documentation about Medicaid EPSDT funding and how it can be obtained in all 50 US States (in 33 States, *regardless of family income)*. It is long past time to throw back the suffocation blanket that has been held on top of Medicaid EPSDT funding by a surprisingly wide range of entities for more than five decades.

The Issachar Project
iss'-ah-kar

Please write to *issachar@ibc-pa.org*
for information about purchasing the new book
The Issachar Project

Steven Kossor

The children of Issachar were trusted advisors because
"they understood the times, and knew what to do."

The Issachar Project was created in Phoenix, Arizona on February 21, 2009 when I addressed a group of about 70 people who had gathered to learn more about the fantastic resources that exist within the Medicaid system to fund behavioral treatment for children with Autism and other disorders anywhere in the USA using the Early and Periodic Screening, Diagnosis and Treatment (EPSDT) funding mandate *regardless of family income in 33 States.*

This book is an essential resource that explains in detail how to navigate the bureaucracy obscuring access to EPSDT treatment funding for children under the age of 21 in the USA. Practitioners can implement the treatment concepts and strategies described here that have been tested successfully for more than 20 years for the benefit of children they are treating anywhere in the world.

380 full-size pages with illustrations and documentation of State and Federal standards for the delivery of EPSDT funded mental health treatment and behavioral support for children based on the author's successful implementation in Pennsylvania since 1992.

Visit http://www.ibc-pa.org/the_issachar_project.htm for more information.

Visit www.TreatmentPlansThatWorked.com to obtain real-life treatment plans that were successfully funded through EPSDT in Pennsylvania, with the data that documents their effectiveness. In over 10 years, just one person has requested a refund for this purchase.

Visit www.ibc-pa.org for information about the Institute for Behavior Change, our values, our history and other useful information. We are a 501-c-3 nonprofit Foundation and can teach others about our successful treatment model and outcome measurement methods that maximize the probability of obtaining and retaining treatment funding.

www.ingramcontent.com/pod-product-compliance
Lightning Source LLC
Chambersburg PA
CBHW050909290526
45792CB00002B/752